Easy Recipes
Easy Chinese

我爱中国菜 吉暐 编著

Dear Arlene,

I'm glad we met
and become good friends.
Enjoy this book!

Jessica
Jan. 23, 2015

华语教学出版社
SINOLINGUA

First Edition 2009
Fourth Printing 2014

ISBN 978-7-80200-644-7
Copyright 2009 by Sinolingua Co., Ltd
Published by Sinolingua Co., Ltd
24 Baiwanzhuang Road, Beijing 100037, China
Tel: (86)10-68320585 68997826
Fax: (86)10-68997826 68326333
http://www.sinolingua.com.cn
E-mail: hyjx@sinolingua.com.cn
Facebook: www.facebook.com/sinolingua
Printed by Dachang Integrity Printing Co., Ltd

Printed in the People's Republic of China

About the Author

The author is many things to many people: philosopher, diplomat, social activist. In his private hours, he is a gourmet, and a connoisseur of the finer things in life. Professionally, he has devoted many years to the study of international affairs and has become a leading expert in the field. He graduated from Fudan University, and completed his PhD courses at Harvard University. Once awarded the title of Outstanding Young Teacher, he also took part in the design of Shanghai International Conference Centre. Being the President of an international media group, he also holds important positions in the Shanghai Gastronomy Association, the Chinese People's Association for Friendship with Foreign Countries, the Chinese People's Institute of Foreign Affairs, China International Public Relations Association, and the All-China Federation of Returned Overseas Chinese.

The author of this book has had many rich experiences in life, from working in coal mines to studying in some of the best universities in the world, and has showcased his talents in many fields.

Preface

--○

Lao Zi, an ancient Chinese philosopher, once said, "'Governing a great nation is much like cooking a small fish."

From the art of cooking, the philosopher learned the principle of governing a state. Though seemingly unrelated fields, cooking and governing share one common tenet — don't stir it too often.

Food is an essential part of Chinese culture. Cooking Chinese food, one can taste the delicacies of China, acquaint oneself better with its culture, and feel the inspiration drawn from learning more about this millennia old civilization.

In terms of cuisine, there is a considerable difference between China and the West. Chinese cuisine can be much more individualized and impulsive than Western cuisine. Although there are recipes to follow, cooks frequently adjust the seasonings and even ingredients they use, according to the preferences and wishes of their customers, which makes each dish creatively unique. Take the cold dish Flavored Cucumber as an example. The flavor of this simple, cold dish differs from place to place, depending on local tastes. People in Shanxi Province (in North China) like vinegar, so they will add more vinegar to the dish; people in Sichuan Province (in southern China) prefer spicy foods, so naturally they will prepare this dish with more chilies; people in Jiangsu Province (in eastern China) enjoy sweet foods, and therefore sugar will be the seasoning of choice for this dish. Though the style of cuisine may vary from place to place, the pursuit of taste remains the main aim of every region.

Familiar with recipes that list specified quantities of ingredients, Westerners may feel confused when running into units of measurement such as "a pinch of", or "to taste" in Chinese recipes. However, this is merely a reflection of the flexibility and creativity used in the art of Chinese cooking. Cooks can add their own desired flavors to the dishes using the recipes as a base; by cooking this way each dish will end up being a unique creation.

Thanks to globalization, a growing number of Chinese are now enjoying Western-style food; at the same time Chinese food is enjoying wider popularity among people in the West. For some, Chinese cuisine may appear to be rather exotic and mysterious. Actually, for most Chinese dishes the ingredients and seasonings are simple and readily available; the preparation of the dish itself is also relatively easy. You don't need to be Chinese to cook a tasty Chinese meal!

Hopefully, this book can introduce foreigners to the wonderful diversity of Chinese food, and offer them a glimpse into Chinese culture.

The editor
August 28, 2009

CONTENTS

Tofu and Cold Dressed Dishes

豆腐、凉菜

Vegetables 蔬菜

Poultry and Eggs 禽蛋

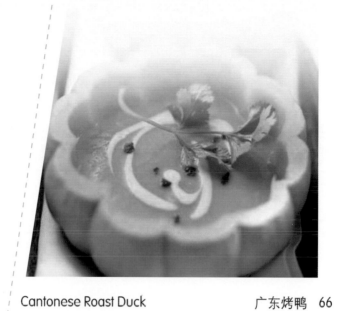

Meat 肉类

Soup/ Dessert/ Staple Food

汤、甜点、主食

炝拌黄豆芽

Qiàngbànhuángdòuyá

(Soybean Sprouts Dressed with Hot Oil)

Ingredients:

250g soybean sprouts; 1 carrot; 2 sprigs of coriander; 10 pieces of Chinese prickly ash; 1/2 tbsp oil; 1 tsp salt; sesame oil to taste

Directions:

1. Thoroughly rinse the soybean sprouts. Peel the carrot and shred finely. Wash the coriander and cut into 3cm long sections.

2. Boil some water in a saucepan. Add the soybean sprouts and blanch for 1 minute, then drain. Blanch the shredded carrot for 20 seconds, and then drain.

3. Place the soybean sprouts, carrot, and coriander into a big bowl. Add the salt and sesame oil, and mix well.

4. Heat the oil and add in the Chinese prickly ash for flavor. Add the oil to the vegetables when hot. Mix well and serve.

Lao Zi Says...

The Chinese philosopher Lao Zi, who is estimated to have lived between 580 BC and 500 BC, once said: "Governing a great nation is much like cooking a small fish." He meant that governing a country required just the right amount of seasoning and care for successful results. This metaphor illustrates the significance that food occupies in Chinese culture.

Liángbànmù'ěr
✳ 凉拌木耳 (Cold Dressed Wood Ear Mushroom)

Ingredients:

A handful of wood ear mushrooms; half each: garlic, red and yellow pepper; 1 tbsp white vinegar; 1 tbsp mature vinegar; salt to taste; 1 tsp sugar; 1 tsp chili oil; 1/4 tsp sesame oil

Directions:

1. Soak the wood ear mushrooms in warm water and add some cornstarch to clean them.

2. Heat water in a pot over high heat. Bring to the boil. Blanch the wood ear mushrooms for three minutes. Remove, add cold water and then drain.

3. Tear the wood ear mushrooms into small pieces. Seed the peppers and remove the pedicels and then cut them into 4cm long fine strips. Grate the garlic.

4. Place the wood ear mushrooms, peppers, and garlic into a big bowl. Add the white vinegar, mature vinegar, salt, sugar, chili oil and sesame oil. Blend until mixed well, and then serve.

Tips

Order of Courses in a Chinese Meal

There is an order to follow when it comes to serving a Chinese meal. In a normal meal, cold dishes are the first to be served, followed by hot dishes, main dishes, desserts and soups, and lastly, fruits. Salty desserts should be combined with salty soups, and sweet desserts with sweet soups.

*椒香海带丝*Jiāoxiānghǎidàisī* (Cold Dressed Seaweed Strips with Peppers)

Ingredients:

200g seaweed; 1 chili; 1/2 green pepper; 1/2 red pepper; 3 garlic cloves; 1/2 tsp salt; 1 tsp sugar; 1 tbsp vinegar; 1/2 tsp light soy sauce; 1/2 tsp sesame oil

Directions:

1. Seed the chili, green and red peppers and cut them into fine strips. Soak in water for 10 minutes or until the strips become curly. Rinse the seaweed and cut it into fine strips. Grate the garlic.

2. Heat water in a pot and bring it to the boil. Add the seaweed strips and blanch for 2 minutes. Then soak in cold water, remove, and drain.

3. Place the seaweed, peppers, chili and garlic in a bowl. Add the salt, sugar, vinegar and sesame. Mix well and serve.

Easy Chinese

Wǒ è le.
我饿了。   I'm hungry.

Wǒ kě le.
我渴了。   I'm thirsty.

*爽口芹菜卷(Celery Curls Mixed with Peppers)

Shuǎngkǒuqíncàijuǎn

Ingredients:

2 celery stalks; half each: red and yellow peppers; 1/2 tsp salt; 1/2 tsp sugar; 1 tsp white vinegar; 1/2 tsp sesame oil

Directions:

1. Seed the red and yellow peppers, and cut them into fine strips. Soak in water for more than 10 minutes.

2. Cut the celery stalks into 5cm long sections and divide each section horizontally into two. Soak in water until they become curly.

3. Heat water in a pot over high heat. Then turn off the heat, add the celery and blanch for 20 seconds. Remove and soak in cold water to cool. Remove and drain.

4. Place the celery, red and yellow peppers in a bowl and add sugar, salt, white vinegar and sesame oil. Blend and serve.

Easy Chinese

kuàizi 筷子	chopsticks	bēizi 杯子	glass/cup
sháozi 勺子	spoon		
chāzi 叉子	fork		
dāo 刀	knife		

Sàixiāngguā

✳赛香瓜 (Cucumber and Pear Salad)

Ingredients:

1 cucumber; 1 pear; 1 piece of hawthorn cake; 1/4 tsp salt; 1 tbsp honey

Directions:

1. Wash the cucumber and peel the pear. Then shred the cucumber, pear, and hawthorn cake finely. Put the cucumber and pear into a large bowl, add the salt and honey then marinate for 20 minutes (covered with cling film).

2. Place the cucumber and pear mix onto a plate, garnish with the finely shredded hawthorn cake and serve.

Tips

Components of a Chinese Meal

A Chinese meal typically consists of two or more general components: A carbohydrate source, known as 主食 (zhǔshí main food, staple) in the Chinese language, such as rice, or wheat-based products, including noodles and steamed buns; and accompanying dishes of vegetables, meat, fish, or other items, known as 菜 (cài dish) in the Chinese language.

Bànhuángguā

✳拌黄瓜 (Flavored Cucumber)

Ingredients:

500g gherkins (baby cucumber); 4g salt; 1 tbsp sesame oil

Directions:

1. Clean the gherkins and remove both ends. Halve them and then slice them into strips. Place them in a dish and add 3g salt. Blend well and set aside for about 1 hour.

2. Squeeze the gherkins, dry and return them to the dish. Add sesame oil, 1g salt and mix well. Serve.

Tips

The History of Chopsticks

Chopsticks are the primary eating utensil in China. While the precise origins of chopsticks are unknown, they have been the utensil of choice throughout China since the Han Dynasty (approximately 200 BC to 200 AD).Their enduring popularity since then may be attributed to Chinese cooking methods—food is usually cut into tiny pieces, making it easy to manipulate with chopsticks.

Liángbànbáicài

✳凉拌白菜(Chinese Leaf and Carrot Salad)

Ingredients:

200g Chinese leaf; 100g carrot; salt, sesame oil, and vinegar to taste

Directions:

1. Rinse the Chinese leaf, and cut or tear it into small pieces. Peel the carrot and cut it into fine strips.

2. Add salt, sesame oil, and vinegar to the Chinese leaf and carrot. Mix well and serve.

Easy Chinese

Wǒ chībǎo le.
我 吃 饱 了。　　　I'm full.

Wǒ chī bu xià le.
我 吃 不 下 了。　　I can't eat anymore.

Hǎitáidòufu

* 海苔豆腐 (Tofu with Nori)

Ingredients:

A block of tofu; a handful of nori; 1 tsp each: shredded green pepper, shredded red pepper; 1 tbsp soy sauce; 1/2 tsp sugar; coriander to garnish

Directions:

1. Mix the soy sauce with the sugar and blend well to make the sauce.

2. Place the block of tofu on a plate and sprinkle it with sauce. Cut the coriander into big pieces and place it around the tofu as garnish.

3. Add the nori, and shredded green and red peppers to the top of the tofu.

Tips

Vegetarianism

Vegetarianism is not unusual in China. In ancient China, many sages believed vegetarian food was nourishment both for people's minds and bodies. The spread of Buddhism promoted vegetarian food amongst laymen. The cuisine of vegetarian food was thus developed. There are many Chinese imitation meat dishes resembling meat dishes in shape and in taste.

Mápódòufu
✳ 麻婆豆腐 (Mapo Tofu)

Ingredients:

200g tofu, 100g beef mince; 15g spring onion, grated

Seasonings:

4 tsp broad bean paste; 2 tsp each: fermented black beans, soy sauce, minced ginger; 0.5g chili powder; 1.5g fried Chinese prickly ash; 1g salt, 5g sugar; 1/2 tsp cornstarch solution; 10 tbsp chicken soup; 5 tbsp oil

Directions:

1. Cut the tofu into 2cm cubes. Boil them in water for a few minutes. Remove, and soak in water.

2. Add oil to a preheated pan. Stir-fry the beef mince until golden. Add broad bean paste and stir-fry.

3. Add fermented black beans, ginger, chili powder and stir-fry until the beef is seasoned. Add the tofu and the chicken soup, then boil over mild heat for a while. Add the soy sauce, spring onion, sugar and salt.

4. Thicken with cornstarch solution. Sprinkle with fried Chinese prickly ash, and serve with rice if you like.

Tips

Food Preparation

First of all, you don't need a cleaver to cook Chinese food; any sharp knife can be used to prepare the ingredients. Ingredients should be cut into pieces of equal size, so that they will be cooked evenly. Always cut beef across the grain, as this helps make it tender.

Ròumòdòufu

✳肉末豆腐(Tofu with Minced Pork)

Ingredients:

600g tofu; 150g pork, minced; 2 tsp soy sauce; 3g salt; 1/2 chicken stock cube; 1 tsp rice wine; 5g ginger, grated; 3g spring onion, cut finely; 1g ground pepper; 2 cups of chicken stock; 5 tsp cornstarch solution; 3 tbsp cooked lard

Directions:

1. Cut the tofu into one inch cubes. Place it in the boiling water. Add a pinch of salt. Remove when boiled.

2. Add the lard to a pre-heated wok. Stir in the pork, ginger, rice wine, stock, soy sauce, salt, and ground pepper. Bring to the boil.

3. Thicken with cornstarch solution. Sprinkle the chicken stock cube, spring onion and lard on top of the dish. Serve.

xīhóngshì 西红柿	tomato	juǎnxīncài 卷心菜	cabbage
tǔdòu 土豆	potato		
húluóbo 胡萝卜	carrot		
yángcōng 洋葱	onion		

Zhádòufu

✳炸豆腐 (Deep Fried Tofu)

Ingredients:

2 blocks of tofu, sliced; 5 cups of peanut oil

Dipping sauce:

3 tbsp soy sauce; 1 tsp white rice wine vinegar; 1 tsp sugar; 1/2 tsp chili, chopped finely; 1 stalk of spring onion, chopped; 1 garlic clove, grated; a pinch of pepper

Directions:

1. Rinse and drain tofu.

2. Mix dipping sauce ingredients in a bowl, and stir, making sure the sugar is dissolved. Place it in individual dishes.

3. Heat oil in a wok or pot to about 180°C. Fry the tofu quickly until golden brown. Remove and drain well.

4. Serve immediately. Dip tofu into sauce for flavor.

Tips

The Pursuit of Taste

Taste is the ultimate goal of Chinese cuisine. In most Chinese dishes, food is prepared in bite-sized pieces. This way, the food will be well seasoned, and thus very tasty. However, fish is usually cooked and served whole to preserve its freshness. The most common compliment made to a cook will be 好吃 (hǎo chī the food is tasty).

✳ 甜酸豆腐 (Sweet and Sour Tofu)

Ingredients:

2 blocks of tofu; 1/3 green bell pepper, shredded; 2 chilis, shredded; 1/2 cup oil; cherry tomatoes to garnish (optional)

Seasonings:

2 tbsp each: ketchup, vinegar, water; 1 tsp each: chili sauce, sugar

Directions:

1. Deep fry the tofu over high heat. Remove.

2. Leave 1 tbsp oil and stir-fry the green pepper and chili for 30 seconds. Add the seasonings and stir.

3. Return the tofu to the pan. Stir until well coated. Garnish with cherry tomatoes if you like.

Tips

The Presentation of Food

In a Chinese meal, each individual diner is given his or her own bowl of rice while the accompanying dishes are served in communal platters. Having everybody sitting around the table and sharing the dishes makes the meal as much an occasion to socialize as it is an opportunity to fill one's stomach!

Suànxiānghélándòu

✳蒜香荷兰豆 (Sautéed Snow Peas with Garlic)

Ingredients:

250g snow peas; 3 garlic cloves, grated; 1 tsp salt; 1 tbsp oil

Directions:

1. Trim and clean the snow peas, then blanch them in boiling water for 20 seconds. Remove and soak in cold water to cool. Remove and drain.

2. Heat the oil in a wok and stir-fry the garlic until fragrant, then stir-fry the snow peas for about one and a half minutes. Sprinkle with salt and mix well.

Tips

Features of Chinese Dishes

Most Chinese dishes are cooked with meat and vegetables, so they contain less calories and are less rich than Western style food. Vegetables stay fresh and crisp by cooking them for a short time over high heat, either in their own juices or in a small amount of water. This method retains most of the vitamins and minerals of the vegetables.

Gānbiānyuánbáicài

✳ 干煸圆白菜 (Stir-Fried Cabbage)

Ingredients:

450g cabbage, sliced into bite sized pieces; 2 tbsp sugar; 2 tbsp white vinegar; 2 tbsp soy sauce; 1 tsp salt; 1/4 tsp ground cayenne pepper; 1 tbsp vegetable oil

Directions:

1. Blend the sugar, vinegar, soy sauce, salt, and cayenne pepper until mixed thoroughly.

2. Add the vegetable oil to a preheated wok over high heat, and heat for 30 seconds.

3. Turn the heat down to a moderate level. Add the cabbage and stir-fry for 3 minutes until it is wilted and coated with oil.

4. Remove the wok from the heat and stir in the sauce mixture. Serve immediately.

Easy Chinese

bōcài 菠菜	spinach	lúsǔn 芦笋	asparagus
jiāng 姜	ginger	wōjù 莴苣	lettuce
suàn 蒜	garlic		
dòufu 豆腐	tofu		

Gānbiāndòujiǎo

✳干煸豆角 (Stir-Fried String Beans)

Ingredients:

300g string beans, trimmed; 100g pork, cut into strips; 1 tbsp minced garlic; 1/4 tsp salt; 1½ tbsp oil for frying; red pepper and sesame oil to taste.

Directions:

1. Cut the string beans into 2-inch long strips. Slice the red pepper into fine strips. Heat the oil and stir-fry the garlic until fragrant. Add the pork and stir-fry.

2. Add the string beans and stir-fry briefly.

3. Add 1/4 cup of water, salt, pepper and sesame oil, then cover and cook until steamed. Cook for another 2 minutes. Serve immediately

Tips

Cooked and Hot Food

The Chinese are very devoted to both cooked and hot food. The discovery of how to use fire for cooking marked the end of Chinese people eating uncooked food. Fire was originally used to simply bake and roast food, but by the period of the Yellow Emperor, people had begun to learn to cook by steaming and boiling. Chinese recognize that well-cooked food is more appetizing and fragrant.

Jīdànxīhóngshì

✳ 鸡蛋西红柿 (Stir-Fried Eggs with Tomatoes)

Ingredients:

3 eggs, whisked; 300g tomatoes; 3 garlic cloves, minced

Seasonings:

3/4 tsp salt; 1/2 tsp sugar; a pinch of ground white pepper

Directions:

1. Cut the tomatoes into eighths. Heat 1 tbsp of oil in a pan over medium heat. Pour in the egg mixture, and stir continually until the eggs are set.

2. Sauté the minced garlic with 1 tbsp of oil until fragrant. Add tomatoes and stir-fry until their juices begin to release.

3. Add 1 tbsp of water, and cover the pan. Simmer for 3 minutes. Toss in the cooked eggs and add all the seasonings. Stir until mixed well. Serve immediately.

Tips

"Enjoy the Meal!"

When Chinese hosts entertain guests for dinner, they usually say: "慢慢吃 (mànmān chī literally, eat slowly)!" A foreign guest may find it quite confusing: Why "eat slowly"? In fact, this is a polite expression used to encourage the guests to feel at home. There is no need for guests to slow down the speed of their dining when this is said. Just enjoy the meal!

Ròumòshāoqiézi

✳ 肉末烧茄子 (Sautéed Eggplant with Minced Pork)

Ingredients:

2 long eggplants; 100g pork, minced; 2 green peppers, sliced into small pieces; 2 red peppers, sliced into small pieces; 1 tbsp finely chopped spring onion; 1 tbsp grated ginger; 1 tsp cooking wine; 1 tbsp sweet soybean paste; 2 tbsp bean paste; 1 tbsp black bean sauce

Directions:

1. Add the cooking wine and sweet soybean paste to the pork. Add the ginger, mix well and marinate for 10 minutes.

2. Remove the pedicels of the eggplants and section them into pieces. Heat oil in a wok and add the eggplants. Stir-fry until the eggplants become soft. Remove.

3. Leave enough oil to cover the bottom of the wok. Stir-fry the pork until its color changes. Remove the pork from the center of the wok and stir-fry the bean sauce and black bean sauce until fragrant. Then mix with the minced pork.

4. Add the eggplants and green and red peppers. Stir-fry until evenly mixed. Serve.

Easy Chinese

Zhēn hǎo chī.
真 好 吃。　It's very tasty.

Hǎo chī jí le.
好 吃 极 了!　It's absolutely delicious!

Suànróngjiāngdòu
✳蒜蓉豇豆 (Garlic Cowpea)

Ingredients:

500g cowpea; 5 garlic cloves, crushed; 1 tbsp oil; 1 tsp salt;
2 tsp oyster sauce; 1/4 tsp sugar

Directions:

1. Remove both ends of the cowpea, clean and section.

2. Heat oil in a wok over high heat. Stir-fry 3/4 of the garlic until fragrant.

3. Add in the cowpea and stir-fry briefly. Stir in salt. Then turn the heat down to medium. Cover and heat for 2 minutes, tossing occasionally.

4. Add in the remaining garlic, oyster sauce and sugar, and stir-fry for about 2 minutes. When the cowpea is cooked, serve.

Tips

Food is Better than a Medicinal Remedy

The kind, and amount of food one eats is relevant to one's health. Chinese people believe that nutritious food is better than a medicinal remedy. Food not only affects one's health as a general principle, but the selection of the right food also depends upon one's state of health at that time. Food, therefore, is occasionally regarded as medicinal.

Xiānggūyóucài

✳ 香菇油菜(Mushrooms and Bok Choy)

Ingredients:

1 small onion, sliced; 1 tbsp garlic, minced; a small portion of ginger, sliced; 6-8 whole Chinese black mushrooms, cleaned, soaked and drained (keep the water); 1 small bunch of bok choy, cut in to bite sized pieces; 2 tbsp oyster sauce; 1 tsp light soy sauce; salt and ground pepper to taste; 1½ to 2 cups of water; 1-2 tsp vegetable oil; 1 chicken stock cube

Directions:

1. Heat the vegetable oil in a pan. Stir-fry the onion and garlic.

2. Add the Chinese black mushrooms and cook until they become tender. Add the bok choy, the soy sauce and oyster sauce, while stirring constantly.

3. Add the water in which the mushrooms were soaked. Stir and then add the chicken stock cube. Stir again to make sure it dissolves properly. Add salt and pepper, if needed.

4. Simmer for 3 minutes and serve.

Easy Chinese

jīròu 鸡肉	chicken	yú 鱼	fish
niúròu 牛肉	beef	dàn 蛋	egg
yángròu 羊肉	lamb		
zhūròu 猪肉	pork		

Sōngrényùmǐ

* 松仁玉米 (Sautéed Sweet Corn with Pine Nuts)

Ingredients:

350g sweet corn kernels; 100g pine nuts; 1 tbsp cornstarch solution; 10g spring onion, chopped; 2g salt and 1/2 chicken stock cube; 1 tsp rice wine; oil for frying

Directions:

1. Heat oil to 110℃. Add the pine nuts and deep fry until they become golden. Remove and drain the oil.

2. Mix together the salt, chicken stock cube and chopped onion and set aside.

3. Heat 2 tbsp of oil in the wok. Add the sweet corn and the seasoning mixture. Bring these ingredients to the boil and then add the pine nuts.

4. Thicken with the cornstarch solution and serve.

Eight Regional Cuisines

There are eight regional cuisines in China: those of Anhui, Guangdong, Fujian, Hunan, Jiangsu, Shandong, Sichuan, and Zhejiang. There are also many Buddhist and Muslim sub-cuisines. The differences in culinary practices between the cuisines largely result from the varying climates and availability of food in different regions.

Jiàngzhīchǎoxiānmó

✳ 酱汁炒鲜蘑 (Sautéed Mushroom)

Ingredients:

500g Chinese mushrooms, chopped into thick pieces; a half each: red and green pepper, shredded roughly; 2 tbsp butter; 1 tbsp oil; 2 tbsp soy sauce; 1 tsp brandy

Directions:

1. Heat the wok, and add the oil and the butter. After the butter melts, add the mushroom pieces and stir well over medium heat.

2. When the mushroom pieces are softened, add the soy sauce, and then add all the roughly shredded peppers, continuously stirring the mixture for about half a minute.

3. Pour the brandy over the dish and serve.

Tips

Blanching

Blanching is often used to cook fresh vegetables as it allows them to maintain their color and texture. Foods to be blanched are cooked by plunging them into boiling water, and removing them after a brief, timed interval.

Jīròuxiānggūhùishíjǐn

*鸡肉香菇烩什锦

(Braised Chicken with Chinese Black Mushrooms and Vegetable Mix)

Ingredients:

250g chicken breast; 6 Chinese black mushrooms; 1 carrot, peeled and cut into cubes; 200g peas; 1 tsp chopped scallion; 1 tsp grated garlic; 1 tbsp cooking wine; 1 tbsp cornstarch solution; 1 tsp salt; 1 tbsp soy sauce; 1 tsp sugar; 1/4 tsp each: chicken stock cube, sesame seeds; oil for frying

Directions:

1. Rinse and cut the chicken into cubes. Add the cooking wine and cornstarch solution and blend well. Marinate for 10 minutes.

2. Peel the peas, then rinse and drain them. Soak the mushrooms in salt water for 10 minutes and then cut them into cubes.

3. Heat the wok over high heat for 20 seconds and pour in the oil. When the oil is hot, add in the chicken cubes, and stir-fry. Remove when the color changes.

4. Heat oil in the wok and stir-fry the scallion, ginger, and garlic until fragrant. Add in the carrot, peas and mushrooms, and stir-fry for 3 minutes. Add the soy sauce, salt, sugar and mix. Add the chicken stock cube and stir-fry for another minute, then turn off the heat. Sprinkle with sesame seeds and serve.

Easy Chinese

mǐfàn 米饭	(cooked) rice		chūnjuǎn 春卷	spring roll
jiǎozi 饺子	Chinese dumpling/jiaozi			
mántou 馒头	steamed bread			
miàntiáo 面条	noodles			

Shānhúbáicài

* 珊瑚白菜 (Coral Chinese Leaf)

Ingredients:

500g Chinese leaf; 5g red and green peppers, shredded; 3 tsp sesame oil; 100g sugar; 3 tbsp rice vinegar; small amount of salt and shredded ginger to taste

Directions:

1. Rinse the Chinese leaf and get rid of the old leaves. Slice the Chinese leaf into fine strips.

2. Marinate the Chinese leaf in salt water for 30 minutes. Remove and drain.

3. Add sugar to the rice vinegar and pour the mixture over the Chinese leaf. Marinate for 2 to 3 hours.

4. Stir-fry the shredded ginger and pepper in the sesame oil until fragrant. Add the Chinese leaf and blend well. Serve immediately.

Tips

Yin and Yang in Chinese Cooking

To the Chinese, yin represents the dark, feminine, damp, mild, and cool elements. Yang, on the other hand, represents the bright, masculine, dry, and strong elements. The Chinese believe a harmonious and healthy life is achieved by complementing and contrasting the yin and the yang elements. Eating a balanced meal means using an even combination of yin and yang ingredients and cooking methods.

Chǎosìshū
✳炒四蔬 (Four Precious Vegetables)

Ingredients:

4 tbsp vegetable oil; 100g canned bamboo shoots, drained and shredded into 2.5cm pieces; 100g carrots, peeled and diced; 100g fresh mushrooms, quartered; 100g together: mangetout, peas, French beans; 1 tsp salt; 1 tbsp sugar; 1 tbsp sesame oil

Directions:

1. Heat the oil in a wok. Stir-fry the bamboo shoots and carrots for about 1 minute.

2. Mix the remaining vegetables, salt and sugar. Stir-fry together for about one and a half minutes. Drizzle with sesame oil and serve.

Easy Chinese

Tài là (tián, suān) le!
太辣（甜、酸）了！　It's too spicy (sweet, sour)!

yǒudiǎnrxián (dàn).
有点儿咸（淡）。　It's a bit salty (bland).

Háoyóushēngcài

✳ 蚝油生菜 (Braised Lettuce in Oyster Sauce)

Ingredients:

500g lettuce; 3 tbsp oyster oil; 1 red pepper, chopped; 1 tsp each: grated scallion, grated ginger, cooking wine, salt; oil for frying

Directions:

1. Rinse the lettuce and slice roughly.

2. Heat the oil in a wok. Add the scallion, ginger, red pepper and stir-fry until fragrant.

3. Add the lettuce and stir-fry. Pour in the cooking wine, add salt and stir well. Sprinkle with oyster oil and serve.

Tips

Food and Feng Shui

Feng shui suggests that both the food we eat and ourselves are interrelated, and influence each other. Harmony and balance is an important aspect of the relationship between food and feng shui. It is important that we eat balanced foods, which consists of a variety and balance of colors. Feng shui recommends that a dish should contain different colors which are in harmony with each other.

✳地三鲜(Sautéed Potato, Green Pepper and Eggplant)

Ingredients:

150g eggplants, rinsed and cut into oblique pieces; 100g potatoes, peeled and diced; 50g bell red pepper, diced; 50g green pepper, diced; 3 tsp vegetable oil; 2 tsp soy sauce; 3g sugar; 5g scallion, chopped; 5g garlic, minced; 2g salt; 30ml cornstarch solution

Directions:

1. Heat the oil until hot. Fry the potatoes until golden, then remove.

2. Fry the eggplants for 3 to 5 minutes. Then add the peppers and fry briefly. Remove.

3. Stir-fry the scallion and garlic in 1 tbsp oil until fragrant. Add the eggplants, potatoes, peppers and stir in the seasonings. Stir-fry briefly and sprinkle with cornstarch solution.

Tips

Seasoning/Marinating

Pork, beef, lamb and chicken need to be seasoned and marinated to add flavor to the dishes, as this will affect their quality. The seasoning process involves first washing the cut meat, then adding it to a mixture of salt, cooking wine, cornstarch and whatever other seasonings the recipe may require, and blending it thoroughly until the meat is completely coated in the mixture.

Fúróngdàn

*芙蓉蛋(Chinese Egg Foo Yung)

Ingredients:

6 eggs, beaten; 1 cup broccoli florets; soy sauce to taste; 1/2 cup chopped ham; 3 spring onions, chopped; oil for cooking

Gravy Mix:

1 cup of chicken soup; 1/2 can of water; soy sauce to taste; small amount of cooked, chopped chicken or other meat

Directions:

1. Mix eggs, broccoli florets, sauce, onions and meat.

2. Heat enough oil to grease the pan, drop the mixture into it by spoon, like pancakes, and fry until light brown on both sides.

3. Remove, place on a heated plate. Keep warm.

4. Heat "gravy mix" until warmed through. Place 3 pancakes on the plate, and cover them with gravy. Add soy sauce to taste.

Tips

Eggs

Eggs hold a special symbolic significance in many cultures, and China is no exception. The Chinese believe eggs symbolize fertility. After a baby is born, parents may hold a "red egg party", where they pass out hard boiled eggs. In some regions of China the number of eggs presented depends on the sex of the child: an even number for a girl, an odd number for u boy.

Lúsǔndànbǐng

*芦笋蛋饼 (Vegetable Jewel Omelet)

Ingredients:

Omelet Mix: 10 large fresh eggs; 1½ cups water

Vegetable Jewel Mixture: 450g bamboo shoots, chopped; 14 spring onions, chopped; 200g red peppers, chopped; 100g asparagus, chopped; 450g button mushrooms, sliced; 1 cup sesame oil; 2 cups stir fry sauce of choice

Directions:

1. Whisk together the eggs and water to prepare the omelet mix.

2. Stir-fry the vegetables (bamboo shoots, spring onion, peppers, asparagus, button mushrooms) until half done.

3. Add sesame oil and the stir fry sauce to the vegetables. Cook for 2 minutes and the vegetable jewel mixture is ready.

4. Prepare 2 egg omelets by using the omelet mix. Fill with a cup of vegetable jewel mixture. Serve.

Easy Chinese

píngguǒ 苹果	apple	xīguā 西瓜	watermelon
chéngzi 橙子	orange		
xiāngjiāo 香蕉	banana		
bōluó 菠萝	pineapple		

Gōngbǎojīdīng

✳ 宫保鸡丁 (Kung Pao Chicken)

Ingredients:

250g chicken breast, diced; handful of dried chilies; 50g fried peanuts; 10g spring onion, chopped; 5g ginger, grated; 5g garlic, minced; 1 tsp each: salt, soy sauce, sesame oil; 1/2 tsp cooking wine; 2 tsp each: cornstarch, rice vinegar, sugar, water; 1 cup oil

Directions:

1. Add the cooking wine, cornstarch, and 1/2 salt to the chicken, toss and then marinate for 5 minutes. Mix together the garlic, ginger, 1/2 tsp salt, sugar, rice vinegar, water, and cornstarch as seasoning and put it aside.

2. Heat oil in a preheated wok. Add the chicken and stir-fry until brown. Remove and drain.

3. Leave 1 tsp oil in the wok. Put in the garlic and spring onion and stir-fry until fragrant. Add the dried chili, and fry for about 1 minute.

4. Add the chicken and stir-fry for 3 minutes. Then add the seasoning and stir-fry over high heat for 1 minute. Add the fried peanuts. Mix well and serve.

Tips

The Guest Gets the Best

At a Chinese meal or banquet, the guests are usually fussed over. The guest of honor naturally receives the choicest morsels. For example, with a fish course, the fish head, the most nutritious part, would be left for the guest of honor. The fish will always be laid on a platter in such a way that the fish head points toward the guest of honor.

Làzijīdīng
✳ 辣子鸡丁 (Fried Chicken Cubes with Chili)

Ingredients:

500g chicken, cubed; 30g spring onion stalk, sliced; 20 pieces of dried chili, sectioned; 2 tsp Chinese prickly ash; 1 tbsp sugar; 2 tbsp vinegar; 2 tbsp cooking wine; salt to taste

Directions:

1. Add the cooking wine and salt to the chicken, and mix well.

2. Heat the oil in a wok until hot and stir-fry the chicken. Remove. Stir-fry the chili and Chinese prickly ash until fragrant.

3. Add the chicken, sugar and vinegar, stir-fry for 2 minutes. Pour in 2 tsp water and continue to stir-fry until the liquid has nearly evaporated.

4. Move the chicken from the center of the wok and stir-fry the spring onion stalk with the salt in the middle of the wok. Stir well and fry until the liquid is absorbed.

cǎoméi 草莓	strawberry	níngméng 柠檬	lemon
pútáo 葡萄	grape		
mùguā 木瓜	papaya		
lí 梨	pear		

Jiāoyánjīchì

✳ 椒盐鸡翅(Salt and Pepper Chicken Wings)

Ingredients:

750g chicken wings; 2 tsp each: sectioned spring onion, grated ginger, salt; 4 tsp each: cooking wine, ground pepper; 1/2 cup vegetable oil

Directions:

1. Marinate the chicken wings with the spring onion, ginger, salt and cooking wine for a moment.

2. Heat the wok and pour in the vegetable oil. Heat until hot. Deep fry the chicken wings until their color changes. Remove.

3. Heat the oil and deep fry the chicken wings until crispy and golden. Remove and sprinkle with pepper.

Bottoms Up!

A proverb says, "When like minds meet, there can never be too many cups." At Chinese dinners, people propose many toasts, and the host usually urges the guests to eat and drink more. Occasionally, guests may even be forced to drink against their will. Nowadays better hosts will try to steer clear of urging their guests to drink excessively.

Yāoguǒjīdīng

✳ 腰果鸡丁 (Sautéed Diced Chicken and Cashew Nuts)

Ingredients:

200g chicken, cut into 1/2 inch squares; 1/2 cucumber, peeled and diced; 2 red peppers, seeded and diced; 1 spring onion, sectioned; 100g cashew nuts; 50g carrot, peeled and diced; 1 tbsp cornstarch; 1/2 tbsp soy sauce; 1 tsp cooking wine; 1 tsp salt; 1 tsp sugar; oil for frying

Directions:

1. Add cooking wine and cornstarch to the chicken, and marinate for 10 minutes.

2. Fry the cashew nuts over low heat until they are lightly browned.

3. Heat the oil and stir-fry the spring onion and red peppers until fragrant. Add the chicken, cooking wine, salt and sugar and stir-fry until half cooked.

4. Add the carrot and cucumber, and stir-fry. Add the cashew nuts and mix well.

Wǒ xiǎng xué zuò fàn.
我 想 学 做饭。
I want to learn how to cook.

Hǎo chī ma?
好 吃吗? Is it tasty?

＊广东烤鸭(Cantonese Roast Duck)

Ingredients:

About 1.5kg duck; 2 tsp Chinese five spice powder; 2 tsp salt; 1 tsp anise powder; 1 tsp sugar; 1 tsp maltose; 5 tsp water

Directions:

1. Prepare the duck.

2. Mix the five spice powder, salt, anise powder and sugar together and place the mixture inside the duck. Sew the opening up very securely. Pour a kettle of boiling water over the duck, and then dry it.

3. Boil the 5 tsp water with the maltose, then baste the outside of the duck with it. Hang the duck in a shady airy place for 4 to 6 hours. When the duck is dry, put it in a hot oven (400°F, Gas 6) with a drip tray underneath for 15 minutes. Then reduce the oven temperature to 375°F, Gas 5. Continue cooking for another 45 to 60 minutes.

4. Leave the duck to cool before serving, and chop in into bite-sized pieces.

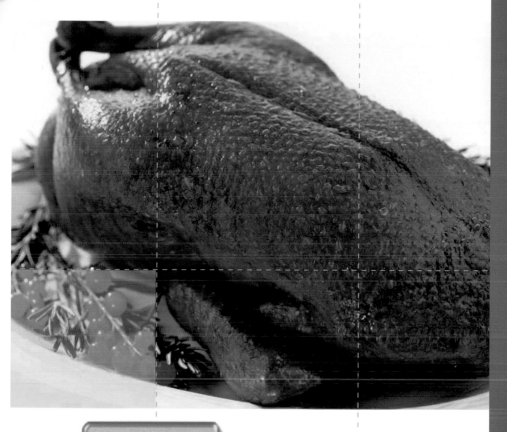

Easy Chinese

yán 盐	salt	fānqiéjiàng 番茄酱	ketchup
táng 糖	sugar		
cù 醋	vinegar		
jiàngyóu 酱油	soy sauce		

✳笋丝炒鸭片 (Stir-Fried Shredded Duck with Bamboo Shoots)

Sǔnsīchǎoyāpiàn

Ingredients:

300g duck, sliced; 450g winter bamboo shoots, sliced; 1 tbsp egg whites; 15g spring onion, minced; 10g ginger, grated; 1 tsp dark soy sauce; 6g salt; 1/2 tsp sesame oil; 1g ground pepper; 15g cooking wine; 15g cornstarch dissolved in 3 tbsp water to make cornstarch solution; 3g sugar; 100ml peanut oil

Directions:

1. Mix the egg and cornstarch solution, and then add the duck. Mix well.

2. Add the sesame oil, sugar, 1g salt, dark soy sauce, and pepper into the mixture. Blend well.

3. Blanch the winter bamboo shoots with 5g salt in boiling water and then drain.

4. Heat the peanut oil to 140°C, and cook the duck until it is half done. Remove the duck and stir-fry the bamboo shoots until cooked.

5. Stir-fry the duck and the rest of the ingredients. Sprinkle some oil on top of the dish before serving.

Tips

General Tips for Cooking With Oil:

When stir-frying with oil, first heat the wok, and then drizzle oil down its sides, so as to coat it in oil. When deep-frying, to judge if the oil is hot enough to start cooking, simply stick a chopstick in the wok. When the oil sizzles around it, you can begin adding the ingredients to the wok.

Cǎijiāochǎoniúròu

✻彩椒炒牛肉 (Stir-fried Beef with Green and Red Pepper)

Ingredients:

150g beef, sliced thinly; 1 green pepper and 1 red pepper, both cut into pieces; 2 spring onions, sectioned; 1 tsp crushed garlic

Marinade:

3/4 tbsp light soy sauce; 1/3 tsp sugar; 1 tsp cornstarch; 1 tbsp oil; 1 tbsp water

Thickening:

A dash of sesame oil and ground pepper; 1 tsp sugar; 1/4 tsp salt; 1 tbsp tomato sauce; 1/2 tsp cornstarch; 3 tbsp water

Directions:

1. Marinate the beef for half an hour.

2. Heat some water in a wok, and bring it to the boil. Parboil the beef and stir. Drain thoroughly when the beef is almost cooked.

3. Heat 1 tbsp of oil in the wok. Stir-fry the green and red peppers, then remove, and put them aside.

4. Heat 2 tbsp of oil in the wok. Stir-fry the beef thoroughly with the garlic before adding the cooked peppers. Pour in the thickening sauce.

Tips

Drinking Etiquette

The host normally refills the guest's glass, but as he is doing so, the guest should put their cup on the table and rest their hand beside it, to show their gratitude. In some southern cities, the guest taps his or her index and middle finger on the table in order to express gratitude.

Gānbiānniúròu
干煸牛肉 (Sichuan-style Crispy Shredded Beef)

Ingredients:

2 eggs; 1/2 tsp salt; 100g cornstarch; 450g topside of beef, sliced into matchstick strips; 1/2 cup vegetable oil; 3 medium carrots, peeled and sliced into matchstick strips; 2 spring onions, cut into 1 inch sections; 2 chilies, shredded; 3 garlic cloves, crushed; 6 tsp sugar; 2 tbsp soy sauce; 4 tbsp wine vinegar

Directions:

1. Blend the eggs, salt, and cornstarch, and toss the beef in the mixture until it is well coated.

2. Heat the oil in a wok, fry the carrots for 2 minutes. Remove and drain.

3. Reheat the oil and deep fry the beef until it is crisp. Remove and drain.

4. Leave about 1½ tbsp of oil in the wok. Reheat. Stir-fry the spring onions, chilies and garlic for about 30 seconds. Then add the sugar, soy sauce and vinegar.

5. Add the beef and carrots to the sauce. Turn off the heat, and serve with rice.

Tips

The Conclusion of a Banquet

At the end of the meal, when everyone has had their ceremonial final cups of tea, the guest of honor should rise. In theory, no other diner can rise until the guest of honor has, and such a social nicety has often resulted in a meal being very lengthy! Nowadays, however, the host will usually give an appropriate, discreet hint to the guest of honor to end the meal.

Qīngtāngdùnniúròu

✳ 清汤炖牛肉 (Clear Simmered Beef)

Ingredients:

900g stewing beef; 3 slices root ginger; 2 tsp salt; 1.75L water; 450g spinach leaves roughly chopped; 1 tbsp chopped coriander

Directions:

1. Cut the beef into 2 inch cubes. Trim away any excess fat.

2. Place the beef in a heavy pan with the ginger, salt and water and boil for a few minutes, then skim.

3. Turn down the heat, cover and simmer very gently for 2½ to 3 hours.

4. Add the spinach to the pan and simmer gently for a further 1 to 2 minutes. Sprinkle with coriander. Serve in individual soup bowls.

Easy Chinese

Zhè shì shénme?
这 是 什么?　　What is it?

Duōshao qián?
多少 钱?　　How much is it?

Suànmiáochǎoniúròu

✳ 蒜苗炒牛肉 (Sauté Beef with Garlic Sprouts)

Ingredients:

150g beef, cut into thick strips; 300g garlic sprouts, sectioned; 10g dried chili; 3g Chinese red pepper; 1 tsp sesame oil; 5g lard; sugar, soy sauce and salt to taste

Directions:

1. Heat the wok and add the lard and sesame oil.

2. Stir-fry the chili and Chinese red pepper until fragrant.

3. Add the beef and stir-fry it with some water. Then add the sugar, soy sauce and salt.

4. Stir in the garlic sprouts and serve.

Tips

Stir-Frying

When stir-frying, you should move the food around the wok, turning it, and tossing it to keep it in motion. By doing this you help the meat, chicken, and vegetables maintain their crispness, flavor, and natural juices, as well as keeping the food from burning. Stir-frying requires you to slice the meat, vegetables, fish, chicken and other foods thinly enough to cook quickly.

Xīlánhuāchǎoniúròu
✳ 西兰花炒牛肉 (Stir-Fried Beef with Broccoli)

Ingredients:

1 broccoli, cleaned and cut; 300g beef tenderloin, cut into
2mm thick slices; 2 garlic cloves; 1 red pepper, sectioned;
1 tbsp cooking wine; 1/2 tsp black soy sauce; 1/4 tsp each:
white and black pepper powder; 1 tbsp cornstarch; 1 tbsp
XO sauce (or lobster sauce); 1/2 tsp salt; 1 tbsp cornstarch
solution; a dash of sesame oil

Directions:

1. Place the broccoli and the beef in a bowl and add the
cooking wine, dark soy sauce, white and black pepper powder, and cornstarch. Marinate for 10 minutes.

2. Heat water in a pot until boiled. Blanch the broccoli for
20 seconds. Remove and drain.

3. Heat oil in a pan over high heat until hot. Stir-fry the
garlic until fragrant. Stir-fry the beef until its color changes.
Stir in the broccoli, XO sauce, salt, pepper and stir-fry. Add
a little water. Ten seconds later, thicken with the cornstarch
solution. Sprinkle the dish with sesame oil and serve.

Easy Chinese

kuàngquánshuǐ 矿泉水	mineral water	
chéngzhī 橙汁	orange juice	
niúnǎi 牛奶	milk	
kāfēi 咖啡	coffee	

Húluóbodùnniúròu

✳胡萝卜炖牛肉(Braised Beef with Carrot)

Ingredients:

500g boned chuck roast or a thick steak, cut into cubes about 1 inch thick; 450g carrot, cut into cubes about 1 inch thick; 1/3 cup dark soy sauce; 1/4 cup Chinese rice wine or dry sherry; 1 spring onion, thinly sliced; 1 tbsp vegetable oil; 3 slices of fresh ginger; 2 garlic cloves, minced; 2 cups water; pepper and salt to taste (optional); 1 tbsp brown sugar; oil for frying

Directions:

1. Combine the dark soy sauce, rice wine or sherry, and spring onion in a small bowl. Set aside.

2. Heat 1 tbsp of oil in a pot over medium heat. Add the ginger and garlic and then the beef. Cook for 4 to 5 minutes to brown the beef. Turn it over at least once.

3. Stir in the soy sauce mixture and cook for a minute. Add the water and bring to a boil. Turn down the heat, cover, and simmer for 1 hour.

4. Add the carrot and stir in the sugar. Simmer uncovered for another 20 minutes. Taste and adjust the seasonings if necessary.

Tips

Chinese Breakfast

Chinese breakfasts are relatively unknown outside China. Perhaps it is because Chinese breakfast is always quick and simple. It may be a bowl of porridge, or soybean milk with steamed stuffed buns, or various steamed or fried dim sum. No matter what kind of breakfast one chooses, it will always be cooked and hot. It's very common in China to have one's breakfast at street vendor stalls.

Tiánsuānròu

✳ 甜酸肉 (Sweet and Sour Pork)

Ingredients:

400g pork tenderloin, cut into 1 inch think slices; 250g cornstarch; 10g spring onion, finely sliced; 10g ginger, finally sliced; 10g sesame seeds; oil for frying; lettuce leaves (optional)

Seasonings:

80g sugar; 5 tbsp vinegar; salt to taste; 2 tsp sesame oil; 3 tsp cooking wine

Directions:

1. Mix the pork slices, cornstarch and water. Blend until the pork is well coated.

2. Mix all the seasonings in a container and put aside.

3. Heat oil in a wok until hot. Fry the slices of pork until golden. Remove.

4. Leave a small amount of oil in the wok and stir-fry the spring onion and ginger until fragrant. Add the seasonings and mix well.

5. Sprinkle the dish with sesame seeds and serve on a plate covered by lettuce leaves (optional).

Tips

Pork as a Synonym for Meat

In China if a dish name includes the word meat, you can be fairly sure that pork is what it includes. For example, in the dish Meat Balls, pork is the meat used. The fact that pork dominates China's meat market may explain how pork became synonymous with meat. Pork accounts for 70 per cent of the meat eaten in China, making China the largest pork consumer in the world.

✳ 糖醋排骨 (Sweet and Sour Spareribs)

Ingredients:

350g pork spareribs, chopped into serving-size pieces; 50g red pepper, cut into small pieces; 100g cucumber, cut into serving-size pieces; 1 garlic clove, sliced; 1 stalk spring onion; salt and pepper to taste; 1/2 cup cornstarch; 1 cup sweet and sour sauce; salad oil

Marinade:

1/3 tsp chicken bouillon; 1 tsp soy sauce; 1/4 tsp white pepper powder; 1 tsp sherry; 1 egg, whisked.

Directions:

1. Place the chopped spareribs into a pot of boiling water and poach for 3-5 minutes. Drain. Combine the marinade ingredients, pour over pork spareribs, and then set aside for 30 minutes.

2. Heat oil in a skillet until hot. Coat the marinated pork spareribs with cornstarch. Deep fry the pork spareribs until golden brown. Remove and drain.

3. Sauté sliced garlic and the white parts of the spring onion until fragrant. Add the red pepper and cucumber and stir briefly.

4. Add the sweet and sour sauce, then the fried pork spareribs and the green parts of the spring onion. Season with salt and pepper. Stir well and serve with pickles and salad if you wish.

Sìxǐwánzi

✳四喜丸子 (Four-Joy Meatballs)

Ingredients:

500g pork, ground; 1 egg; 3 tbsp soy sauce; 2 tbsp cooking wine; 1 tsp minced ginger; 50ml cornstarch solution; 1 tsp finely chopped spring onion; 80ml water; 800ml oil; 1 tsp salt

Directions:

1. Add the chopped spring onion, ginger, 1 tbsp soy sauce, salt, egg and 2 tbsp cornstarch solution to the pork, and blend until the pork becomes sticky.

2. Divide the pork mixture into four pieces and knead them into balls. Gently place the balls in hot oil and fry them until their color changes. Remove and drain.

3. Placed the fried balls in a large bowl and add the remaining soy sauce, cooking wine and the water. Steam over high heat for 15 minutes.

4. Place the balls on a plate. Add the remaining cornstarch solution to the sauce to thicken. Bring to the boil and then pour the sauce over the meatballs. Garnish the plate any way you like.

Tips

Beverages

In Chinese culture, cold beverages are believed to be harmful to the digestion of hot food, so drinks like ice-cold water or soft drinks are not traditionally served at meal-times. Despite this tradition, nowadays beer and soft drinks are popular accompaniments to meals.

Dòuchǐpáigǔ

✳豆豉排骨 (Stewed Spareribs with Black Bean Sauce)

Ingredients:

450g meaty spareribs; 2 tbsp black bean sauce; 1 tbsp rice wine (or dry sherry); 2 tsp cornstarch; 1/2 tsp minced ginger; 2 garlic cloves, minced; 1/4 tsp ground black pepper; 1 tsp cooking oil; 1 tsp sesame oil; 1 tsp sugar; coriander, chopped finally

Directions:

1. Cut the spareribs into 1-inch pieces. Combine the rest of the ingredients. Put the spareribs and the sauce into a shallow, heatproof pan and marinate for 30 minutes.

2. Place the plate of spareribs in a steamer, then cover and steam them in boiling water over medium-high heat for 45 minutes. Before serving, top the dish with some coriander.

Easy Chinese

chá 茶	tea
báijiǔ 白酒	liquor
hóngjiǔ 红酒	red wine
píjiǔ 啤酒	beer

Yúxiāngròusī

*鱼香肉丝(Yu-Shiang Shredded Pork)

Ingredients:

300g pork tenderloin, shredded; 10 wood ear mushrooms; 200g bamboo shoots and carrot, cut into strips; 1 tsp each: grated shallots, grated ginger, grated garlic; 60g chili, chopped; 2 tsp cornstarch solution

Seasoning:

1 tsp soy sauce; 2 tsp vinegar; 1 tsp cooking wine; 1 tsp sugar; 1/2 tsp salt; 1/2 tsp sesame oil; 3 tsp water; 2 tsp cornstarch solution

Directions:

1. Soak and clean the wood ear mushrooms in warm water. Cut into strips.

2. Place the pork in a bowl, and marinate for 5 minutes in the cornstarch solution. Place the shallots and the seasonings in a container to make the sauce and put aside.

3. Pour the oil in to a preheated pan. When the oil is very hot, add the pork and stir-fry until it becomes white. Add the garlic, ginger and chili, stir-fry until fragrant.

4. Add the bamboo shoots, carrot and wood ear mushrooms. Stir-fry for 2 minutes. Add the sauce. Stir-fry for 20 seconds and then serve.

Tips

Deep Frying

Many of the most popular Chinese dishes are deep fried to achieve their crispiness and flavor. Deep frying requires abundant cooking oil in which to submerge the food. The oil is usually heated to about 7/10 hot before the food is added to it. While deep frying, turn the food occasionally to keep it from burning. The most popular types of oil used to deep fry Chinese foods are peanut and sun flower seed oil.

Làròusuànmiáo

✳腊肉蒜苗(Preserved Ham with Garlic Sprouts)

Ingredients:

300g preserved ham; 20g garlic sprouts, sectioned; 30g red pepper, seeded and sliced; 1 tsp sesame oil; 1 tbsp vegetable oil; 2g sugar; 1 tsp cooking wine

Directions:

1. Steam the preserved ham for 20 minutes and then remove. Skin, and cut it into thin slices.

2. Place the preserved ham and garlic sprouts in boiling water until cooked.

3. Pour 1 tbsp oil into the wok and heat. Add the garlic sprouts, red pepper and blend until mixed well. Add the ham, sugar, cooking wine and water, and stir-fry briefly over high heat. Top the dish with sesame oil and serve.

Preserved Food

A notable feature of Chinese food is the large number, and great variety of preserved foods. Food is preserved in various ways, in many kinds of soy sauces, and so forth, and a whole range of foodstuff is involved. With preserved food, the Chinese people are prepared for times of hardship or scarcity.

Hóngshāoròu

✳红烧肉 (Braised Pork)

Ingredients:

500g streaky pork, cut into 2cm thick cubes; 1 Chinese cinnamon stick; 3 bay leaves; 3 pieces of star anise; 5 ginger slices; 1 spring onion, sliced; 2 tbsp dark soy sauce; 1 tsp salt; 6 lumps of rock sugar

Directions:

1. Heat the wok and stir-fry the streaky pork for two minutes over low heat. Then turn them over and stir-fry the other side. Add the soy sauce and stir-fry.

2. When the pork turns dark red, add the spring onion, ginger, rock sugar and just enough boiled water to cover the surface of the ingredients.

3. Add the Chinese cinnamon, bay leaves and star anise. Turn the heat to medium until the mixture has come to a boil. Cover and simmer over low heat for 40 minutes. Add the salt and turn the heat to high. It will be done when the sauce has been absorbed.

Easy Chinese

Wǒ ài Zhōngguócài!
我爱 中国菜！　I love Chinese food.

Wǒ xǐhuan sìchuāncài (shànghǎicài, húnáncài).
我喜欢 四川菜 (上海菜、湖南菜)。
I like Sichuan food (Shanghai food, Hunan food).

Mùxūròu

✳ 木须肉 (Muxu Pork)

Ingredients:

25g wood ear mushrooms; 25g golden needle mushrooms; 100g lean pork; 1/3 cucumber, sliced; 1/2 tsp minced fresh ginger; 1 tsp cornstarch; 2 tsp soy sauce; 3 eggs; 150ml vegetable oil; 1 tsp rice wine; 1 tsp salt; 1/2 tsp sesame oil.

Directions:

1. Wash and soak the wood ear mushrooms. Drain and halve crosswise. Soak the golden needle mushrooms in warm water for 5 minutes and then drain. Put them aside.

2. Wash the pork and slice it into strips. Marinate with the soy sauce, ginger, and cornstarch, and set aside.

3. Whisk the eggs and add 3/4 tsp salt. Scramble the eggs with 5 tbsp of the oil and set aside.

4. Heat 4 tbsp of the oil in a wok over high heat until it's very hot; add the pork strips and stir-fry until partially cooked. Stir in the rice wine. Remove the pork and set it aside.

5. Heat the remaining 1 tbsp oil in the wok. Add the golden needle mushrooms and wood ear mushrooms and stir-fry for 30 seconds. Add 1/4 tsp salt, and cucumber slices. Add the pork strips and scrambled egg. Stir-fry to blend the ingredients. Top with sesame oil, and serve.

Tea

"Better to be deprived of food for three days, than tea for one." —Ancient Chinese Proverb

This proverb shows the importance of tea in the life of the Chinese. The Chinese drink tea for both health and pleasure. Different varieties of tea are believed to have different medical functions. To have a chat with friends over a cup of tea is a true pleasure for the Chinese.

Cōngbàoyángròu

✳ 葱爆羊肉 (Sautéed Mutton Slice)

Ingredients:

300g mutton, sliced; 4 garlic cloves; 1 tbsp white vinegar; 1 tsp sesame oil; 3 green Chinese onions, cut into 5cm long pieces; 1/2 onion, shredded; 3 tbsp oil; 1/2 tsp chicken stock cube; 2 tsp sugar; 2 tsp cornstarch solution; 2 tbsp light soy sauce; 1 tsp cornstarch

Directions:

1. Add the light soy sauce, chicken stock cube and cornstarch to the mutton. Blend and marinate for 10 minutes. Discard the excess sauce and drain. Put aside.

2. Heat 2 tbsp oil in a wok over high heat. When the oil is very hot, quick fry the mutton for 1 minute and then remove.

3. Heat 1 tbsp oil in the wok over high heat. Stir-fry the onion, garlic and green Chinese onion pieces for 2 minutes until fragrant. Add the mutton and stir-fry. Put in the white vinegar, sesame oil, and sugar. Stir-fry for 2 minutes.

4. Pour the ingredients from the wok into a pan. Heat over high heat, and thicken with cornstarch solution.

Easy Chinese

zhuōzi 桌子	table	
yǐzi 椅子	chair	
yáqiān 牙签	toothpick	
cānjīn 餐巾	table napkin	

Wǔwèiyóuyújuǎn
✳ 五味鱿鱼卷(Five-Flavor Squid Rolls)

Ingredients:

1 fresh squid; 5 garlic cloves, crushed; 2 pieces of ginger, grated; 1/2 spring onion, chopped finely; a pepper, grated; a sprig of coriander, chopped finely; 2 tbsp ketchup; 1 tbsp soy sauce; 1/2 tbsp vinegar; pinch of sesame oil.

Directions:

1. Mix everything except the squid together to make the dipping sauce.

2. Remove the head, tail and skin of the squid. Slit open the body, and clean thoroughly. Cut a criss-cross pattern on the body of the squid before cutting it into 1-inch-long pieces. Trim the head and leave it aside.

3. Bring half a pot of water to boil. Then boil the squid for 30 seconds. Remove, and place it on a plate. Serve with the dipping sauce.

The Symbolism of Food

Given the important role food plays in Chinese culture, it is not surprising that many foods have symbolic meanings. The symbolic significance of a food may be based on its appearance, or on how the Chinese word for it sounds. Also, some foods are considered lucky for Chinese people, thus are served on special occasions.

Shànghǎizhēngyú
✳上海蒸鱼 (Shanghai Steamed Fish)

Ingredients:

1 whole fresh carp about 500g (or other fresh water fish); 5 tsp rice wine; 1 tsp salt; 4 Chinese black mushrooms, sliced and soaked; 4 bamboo shoots, sliced; 2 tbsp lean pork, diced and marinated in sugar; 4 slices Chinese ham, steamed; 2½ tbsp vegetable oil; 2 tbsp chopped spring onions; 1 tsp sliced ginger

Directions:

1. Clean the fish and make 2 or 3 X-shaped cuts on each side. Rub with the rice wine and let it marinate.

2. Place the fish on a heat-proof dish and sprinkle it with salt, mushrooms, bamboo shoots and diced pork. Place the ham, spring onions and ginger on top. Drizzle it with vegetable oil.

3. Place the dish in a steamer and steam until the fish is cooked (10 to 15 minutes). Discard the spring onions and ginger, and serve.

Tips

Fish

In China a fish served whole is a symbol of prosperity. In fact, at a banquet it is customary to serve the whole fish last. Fish also has symbolic significance because the Chinese word for fish, 鱼 (yú), sounds like the word for riches or abundance, and it is believed that eating fish will help your wishes come true in the year to come.

Dùnhǎishēn

*炖海参 (Stewed Sea Cucumbers)

Ingredients:

900g sea cucumbers, sliced diagonally; 3 spring onions, sectioned; 4 slices ginger; 1 tbsp shrimp roe; 3 tbsp soy sauce; 1 tbsp sugar; 1 tbsp ginger water; 1 tbsp wine; a dash of sesame oil; 1 tbsp cornstarch; 2 handfuls of broccoli, chopped and boiled (optional); 2 tbsp oil for frying

Directions:

1. Add 1 spring onion, 2 slices ginger, 1 tbsp wine into half a pot of water and bring to the boil. Blanch the sea cucumbers and rinse under cold water. Drain and set aside.

2. Heat 2 tbsp oil. Add the spring onion and ginger. Stir-fry for a while, and then add the sea cucumbers. Fry well.

3. Stir in soy sauce, sugar, water, oil, cornstarch and shrimp roe until well mixed. Place on a dish ringed with broccoli (optional) and serve.

Tips

Spring Rolls

Spring rolls symbolize wealth and prosperity, since their color and shape resemble gold bars. As the name suggests, spring rolls are a dish prepared in celebration of the coming of spring. Originally, they were filled with vegetables. Shrimp and barbecued pork were added later.

Bǎihéxiāqióu

✳ 百合虾球 (Dry Fried Shrimp Balls with Lily Bulbs)

Ingredients:

500g shrimps, shelled, deveined, rinsed and drained. 200g lily bulbs, cleaned and sliced; 150g egg; 5g cornstarch; 7g ginger, grated, 5g garlic, crushed; 5ml cooking wine; 8ml ketchup; 5g salt; 3g sugar; 6ml each: vinegar, soy sauce, sesame oil; 6g sectioned chili; 7ml chili oil; 200ml vegetable oil

Directions:

1. Marinate the shrimps with egg white, cornstarch and water. Set aside.

2. Heat the oil in the wok. Add the shrimps and remove when in the shape of a ball. Add the lily bulbs and remove when cooked.

3. Remove most of the oil. Add the chili and stir-fry until fragrant. Then add the ginger, garlic, cooking wine, water, ketchup, shrimp balls and other seasonings. After the shrimps absorb the sauce, add the lily bulbs and mix well.

Tips

Chicken as Phoenix, and Lobster as Dragon

In China, the phoenix and the dragon are a pair of legendary, mighty animals. Thus they are auspicious symbols. Chicken is referred to as phoenix in some dishes, and is often served with lobster—the symbol of the dragon. Dishes such as these are favorite choices at wedding receptions.

Chǐzhījiānhǎixiā

✳豉汁煎海虾(Shrimps with Black Bean Sauce)

Ingredients:

150g shrimps; 3g garlic, minced; 6g fermented black beans, grated; 2g ginger, crushed; 5g spring onion, chopped; 18ml vegetable oil; 1g salt; 4g cornstarch; a dash of pepper; 50ml chicken stock.

Directions:

1. Add water to the cornstarch to make 8ml cornstarch solution.

2. Heat 15ml oil in a wok. Stir-fry the shrimps until fragrant. Add the garlic, black beans, ginger and chicken stock. Sprinkle with salt and cover the wok.

3. When the shrimp is cooked thoroughly, coat with cornstarch solution. Top it with pepper and 3ml oil, and mix well. Serve.

Easy Chinese

Wǒ chī sù.
我吃素。 I'm a vegetarian.

Wǒ bù chī làjiāo (suàn, bōcài).
我不吃辣椒（蒜、菠菜）。
I don't eat chilies (garlic, spinach).

Chǎosānxiān

✳ 炒三鲜 (Sautéed Mixed Seafood)

Ingredients:

100g prawns, peeled and deveined; 100g scallops, sliced in half; 100g squid, cleaned and sliced; 25g cornstarch; 1 egg white; 2 tbsp vegetable oil; handful of sweet broad peas, stringed; 1 carrot, scraped and cut into diamonds; 2 spring onions, finely chopped; 2.5cm piece of root ginger, peeled and finely chopped; 2 garlic cloves, grated; 100ml chicken stock; 1/2 tsp salt; 1 tbsp dry sherry; a few drops of sesame oil; 1 tsp vinegar

Directions:

1. Mix the prepared prawns with three-quarters of the cornstarch and the egg white. Blend till mixed well.

2. Heat the oil to 180°C. Stir-fry the seafood, sweet broad peas and carrot for about 2 minutes, then remove and drain.

3. Reheat the oil, leaving only enough to coat the bottom of the wok. Then add in the spring onions, ginger, garlic, chicken stock, salt and sherry. Bring to the boil, and then add in the remaining cornstarch and egg white to thicken the sauce.

4. Return the seafood and vegetables to the wok. Sprinkle with sesame oil and vinegar, then mix together and serve hot.

Tips

Round Dining Tables

　　Chinese people have always been partial to dining together, and the dining tables of the Chinese are usually round. There are always several dishes, even in an ordinary meal. Dining together is considered an essential part of a family reunion.

Jiāoyánxiā

* 椒盐虾(Spiced Prawns)

Ingredients:

4 tbsp vegetable oil; 450g prawns, peeled and deveined; 25g coriander, shredded, 15g salt, 25g dried chili, shredded, 50ml peanut oil; 2g spice powder

Directions:

1. Heat the oil in a wok. Add the prawns and stir-fry until almost done. Remove and drain. Pour off all but 1 tbsp of the oil.

2. Stir in the dried chili, then immediately the spice powder and the salt, and mix well.

3. Add the prawns for a few seconds into the chili and spice powder mixture. Stir-fry until done. Pile the prawns onto a dish. Top with coriander and serve.

Tips

Steaming

Steaming Chinese food can involve all sorts of different foods, meat, fish, chicken, vegetables and more. To achieve the best results the water should be constantly on the boil. Also, make sure the food is fresh, and seasoned in advance. High heat, abundant water, and a brief cooking time are the keys to successfully steamed Chinese food.

Huáliūxiārén

✳ 滑熘虾仁 (Stir-fry Shelled Shrimps)

Ingredients:

300g shelled shrimp, deveined; 200g red and yellow peppers; 1 tsp salt; 2 tsp cornstarch; 1 tbsp cooking wine; 1 spring onion stalk, sectioned; 5 slices of ginger, cut into fine strips

Directions:

1. Rinse the shrimps and drain. Add in 1/2 tsp salt, cornstarch, and wine and mix well. Marinate for 10 minutes. Rinse the red and yellow peppers and slice them.

2. Add some oil to the wok and heat until hot. Add in the spring onion, ginger and shrimps and stir-fry them over medium heat. Toss swiftly with a fryer. When the shrimps begin to change color, add in the red and yellow pepper and stir for 2 more minutes. Add the remaining salt and serve.

Special Festive Food

Traditional Chinese holidays are usually associated with a kind of special festive food, may it be *yuanxiao*, *zongzi* or *moon cake*. Each carries its own special meaning related to the festival, and serves to enrich the holidays with delicious flavors and auspicious wishes. Food is an essential part of many festivals.

Bōluóxiārén

✳菠萝虾仁 (Shrimps with Sweet and Sour — Pineapple Sauce)

Ingredients:

About 650g shrimps, shelled; 1/2 cup flour; 1/2 tsp salt; 3 tbsp brown sugar; 1/2 cup pineapple juice; 2½ tbsp vinegar; some chives, sectioned; 1 tbsp cornstarch; 2 eggs, beaten; 50g pineapple pieces; oil for frying; 1/2 a cup of water; 1/4 tsp salt; 2 tbsp ketchup

Directions:

1. Combine the flour and salt. Stir in the eggs and mix well. Coat shrimps lightly with this batter.

2. Fry shrimps until light brown. Place shrimps on a serving platter and garnish with pineapple.

3. Heat the sugar, pineapple juice, vinegar, water, salt, vinegar and ketchup. Then add the chives. Pour the mixture over the shrimps and pineapple.

4. Serve with rice.

Easy Chinese

Wǒ duì hǎixiān (jīdàn, huāshēng) guòmǐn.
我 对 海鲜（鸡蛋、花生） 过敏。
I'm allergic to seafood (eggs, peanuts).

Yǒu kuàngquánshuǐ (píjiǔ, kělè, chéngzhī) ma?
有 矿泉水 （啤酒、可乐、橙汁） 吗?
Do you have bottled water (beer, cola, orange juice)?

Nánguāgēng

✳ 南瓜羹 (Pumpkin Soup)

Ingredients:

1 small pumpkin; 300ml milk; 1 tsp salt; 1/2 white pepper powder; 1/2 onion, minced; 1 tsp oil

Directions:

1. Peel the pumpkin, core it, and slice it into thick strips.

2. Heat the oil in a pan, and stir-fry the onion until fragrant. Add the pumpkin and stir-fry for 3 minutes until its color changes. Pour in cold water and bring to the boil. Simmer the pumpkin for 10 minutes until cooked.

3. Add milk and salt. Simmer for another 5 minutes. Remove and cool for 5 minutes. Put into the blender and blend.

Soup

    Chinese rarely sit down to a lunch or dinner with-
out soup. In contrast to the Western custom of having
soup before the main course, Chinese prefer to enjoy soup
during the meal, or at the end of a meal. Soup is usually served in a deep communal bowl and each individual
ladles their share into their own bowls.

Xiānggūdòufutāng
✳ 香菇豆腐汤 (Chinese Black Mushroom and Tofu Soup)

Ingredients:

10 Chinese black mushrooms, soaked and cut into slices; 100g pork, minced; 1 tofu block, cut into cubes; salt and ground pepper to taste

Directions:

1. Add water to a pot. Bring to the boil. Add the pork with a spoon and stir well.

2. Add the mushrooms and tofu, bring to the boil. Then boil for another 5 minutes. Season with salt and pepper.

Tips

Yuanxiao and the Lantern Festival

The Lantern Festival, the final night of the Chinese New Year holiday, falls on the 15th day of the first lunar month. Yuanxiao, also known as tangyuan, is a typical festive food of the Lantern Festival, and is cooked in boiling water. The main ingredient is glutinous rice flour, and the filling is usually sweet, and can be sesame paste (ground black sesame seeds mixed with sugar and lard) or red bean paste.

Qīngdùnjītāng

✳清炖鸡汤(Clear Chicken Soup)

Ingredients:

350g chicken, chopped into bite-size pieces; 80g carrot, cut into strips; 5g coriander, chopped finely; 1 ginger root, sliced; 8g salt; 5g Chinese prickly ash; 5ml cooking wine; 5ml sesame oil

Directions:

1. Blanch the chicken and drain.

2. Boil a pot of water. Add the sesame oil and ginger. Bring to the boil.

3. Add the chicken, carrot, salt, Chinese prickly ash and cooking wine. Braise for about 1 hour. Sprinkle with coriander and serve.

Tips

Zongzi and the Dragon Boat Festival

The Dragon Boat Festival, falls on the fifth day of the fifth lunar month, and commemorates Qu Yuan—a great poet and loyal political figure of the State of Chu in the third century BC. The preparation and eating of zongzi, a tasty glutinous rice dumpling wrapped in reed leaves with various kinds of fillings, is probably the most wide spread custom of this festival.

Huángguādòufutāng

✳黄瓜豆腐汤 (Gherkin and Tofu Soup)

Ingredients:

100g gherkin, 150g tofu, salt to taste, 1/4 tsp each: chicken stock cube, sesame oil

Directions:

1. Cut the gherkin and tofu into cubes.

2. Heat the wok. Add some water, tofu, salt, and bring to the boil.

3. Add the gherkin, sesame oil and the chicken stock cube. Then serve immediately.

Moon Cakes and the Mid-autumn Festival

Moon cakes are essential during the festival which occurs on the 15th day of the eighth lunar month. This round cake is made of pastry with sweet fillings. Their round shape symbolizes not only the fullness of the moon but also the unity of the family. The family will gather together, chatting, eating cakes, drinking tea or sipping wine under the bright moonlight.

Xìngrénrǔ

* 杏仁乳 (Almond Curd)

Ingredients:

150g finely sliced almonds; 100g agar; 300ml milk; 100g sugar; a few raspberries

Directions:

1. Combine the agar and 100g water in a pot and boil over low heat until the agar is completely melted. Add the milk, the sliced almonds, 50g sugar and mix well as it is being cooked. Take the almond mixture out when it starts to boil and put it in a dish. When it cools off, put it in the freezer to set.

2. Put 500g water in a pot, add the remaining sugar and bring it to the boil. Then put the syrup in the freezer to cool.

3. Take the almond mixture out of the freezer and slice it into bite-size pieces. Put into serving bowls and add the syrup. Add the raspberries.

Tips

Porridge for Laba Festival

On the eighth day of the twelfth lunar month is the traditional Laba Festival. The festival originated from the ritual sacrifice held at the end of the year. The one custom that has managed to survive is the preparation and consumption of a special and nutritious Laba porridge, a food made from a wide variety of grains such as millet, rice, glutinous rice, glutinous millet, beans, and dried nuts and fruit.

Shuāngpínǎi
✳ 双皮奶 (Milk Custard with Double Skins)

Ingredients:

250ml whole milk; 2 tsp white sugar; 2 to 3 egg whites

Directions:

1. Boil the milk over low heat. Pour it into a bowl to cool. Beat the egg whites in another bowl until frothy.

2. After the milk cools, a skin will form on the top of it. Gently lift one point of the skin (so as to keep the whole skin in the original bowl) and pour the milk into the bowl with the egg whites.

3. Add 2 tsp sugar into the milk and egg white mixture. Blend the ingredients, and pour the mixture slowly into the bowl with the milk skin. The skin will surface.

4. Cover the bowl with cling film and steam for 15 minutes over medium heat. It will taste better if refrigerated before serving.

Dessert

In contrast to most Western meals, a Chinese meal does not typically end with a dessert. However, it has become more popular for a sweet dish to be served at the end of a formal dinner or banquet, such as sliced fruits or sweet dim sums.

Báimǐfàn

✳白米饭(Plain Rice)

Ingredients:

2 cups of rice; 3 cups of water

Directions:

1. Rinse and drain the rice.

2. Place the rice into a flat pot with a tight fitting lid. Add water.

3. Bring to the boil over medium heat without the lid. Stir well. Cover with the lid and simmer over a very low heat for about 18 minutes. Turn off the heat and allow the rice to rest for 15 minutes. Serve in individual bowls.

Rice

One of the main staple foods, rice is dominant in southern China. It is hard to exaggerate the importance of rice in Chinese culture. To the Chinese, rice is a symbol of life itself. There are many sayings that demonstrate the status of rice. For example, a person who loses his job is said to have had his rice bowl broken.

✳ 扬州炒饭 (Yang Chow Fried Rice)

Ingredients:

60g shrimps; 60g cooked ham, diced; 2 eggs, beaten lightly; 2 spring onions, finely chopped; 2 tbsp peas; 350g plain cooked rice; 2 tsp salt; pepper to taste; 4 tbsp oil

Directions:

1. Heat a wok with the oil and fry most of the spring onions for 15 seconds. Add the ham and shrimps and stir-fry for 2 minutes.

2. Add the eggs until set and then peas. Stir-fry for another 2 minutes. Stir in the rice and continue to stir-fry for another 3 minutes.

3. Sprinkle with the seasonings and blend well. Garnish with the remaining spring onions.

Qǐng bǎ yán (cù) dìgěi wǒ.

请 把 盐（醋）递给我。

Please pass me the salt (vinegar).

Qǐng gěi wǒ yí fù dāochā (yìshuang kuàizi).

请 给 我一副刀叉（一双筷子）。

A knife and fork (A pair of chopsticks), please.

Bōluófàn

✳菠萝饭 (Pineapple Fried Rice)

Ingredients:

A fresh pineapple; 300g plain cooked rice; 1 egg, beaten; 100g cucumber, cubed; 20g carrot, shredded; 1 spring onion, shredded; 1 tsp salt; 1 tsp light soy sauce

Directions:

1. Cut the pineapple in half lengthways and use one half. Remove the flesh and reserve the shell.

2. Cut the flesh into 1cm thick cubes and place in a bowl. Add in 1/2 tsp salt and cover with water. Soak for 30 minutes and drain.

3. Heat the oil in a wok over high heat until hot and then pour in the egg. Remove when the egg is cooked.

4. Add the oil again and heat over high heat until hot. Add the spring onion, cucumber and carrot, and stir-fry for 1 minute. Add in rice. Press to scatter the rice. Add the egg, pineapple cubes, sprinkle soy sauce and the remaining salt over the top. Stir-fry and mix well.

5. Serve in the pineapple shell.

Tips

Noodles

Noodles are a critical part of Chinese cuisine, particularly in northern China. Noodles are a symbol of longevity in Chinese culture. They are as much a part of a Chinese birthday celebration as a birthday cake with lit candles is in many other countries. The noodles on those occasions are called 长寿面 (chángshòumiàn longevity noodles).

Zhēngxiājiǎo

✳ 蒸虾饺 (Steamed Dumplings with Shrimps)

Ingredients:

500g cornstarch; 100g glutinous rice flour; 250g shelled shrimps; 50g bamboo shoots, shredded; 50g carrots, shredded; 100g pork fat; 1/2 tsp salt; 1/4 tsp sugar; 2 tsp cooking wine; 5g spring onions, finely chopped; 50g lard

Dipping sauce:

1 cup of soy sauce; white vinegar and sugar to taste; 1/2 tsp chili paste; 1/2 tsp each: minced fresh ginger, sesame oil

Directions:

1. Wash, clean, and finely chop the shelled shrimps, bamboo shoots, carrots and pork fat. Add the salt, cooking wine and spring onions and blend well to make the filling.

2. Mix the cornstarch and rice flour with the lard. Add 10 tbsp of boiling water and mix well. Divide into small 20g pieces. Press them into flat wrappings by hand (or use purchased wonton wrappers), put in the filling and seal well.

3. Put them in the bottom of a Chinese steamer with a light coating of vegetable oil. When the water starts to boil, steam for another 10 minutes.

4. Serve on a plate. Place 1 tbsp sauce in individual small bowls for dipping.

Tips

Cooking Vegetables and Meat:

Try to vary the meats and vegetables used in a dish, so that each will have an interesting variety of flavors, textures, and colors. When cooking a meat and vegetable stir-fry, the meat should be cooked separately from the vegetables. The meat should be cooked first and then set aside while the vegetables are stir-fried. The tougher and thicker vegetables will need to be cooked for longer than the softer, leafier vegetables.

Chūnjuǎn

✳ 春卷 (Spring Rolls)

Ingredients:

12 spring roll wrappers; 100g roasted pork, cut into thin strips; 3 dried mushrooms, soaked for about 30 minutes, drained and chopped finely; 1/2 cup mung bean sprouts; 1/2 medium carrot, peeled and shredded; 2 tbsp chopped red bell pepper; 2 tsp dark soy sauce and 2 tsp oyster sauce; 2 tbsp chicken broth; 1/2 tsp sugar; sesame oil to taste; 2 tbsp oil for stir-frying

Directions:

1. Mix the dark soy sauce, oyster sauce, chicken broth, sugar and sesame oil in a small bowl and set aside.

2. Add 2 tbsp oil to a preheated wok over medium heat. When the oil is hot, add the pork and stir-fry for 1 minute. Then add the vegetables and stir-fry for another minute. Push up to the side of the wok. Add the sauce in the middle. Heat briefly and then mix it in with the pork and vegetables. Remove the wok from the heat and allow the filling to cool.

3. Place a roll wrapper with 1 point toward you. Spoon 1/4 cup vegetable filling diagonally across, and just below the center of the wrapper. Fold the bottom corner of the wrapper over the filling and then tuck the point under the filling. Fold the side corners over, forming an envelope shape. Roll up toward the remaining corner, moisten the point and press firmly to seal. Repeat with remaining roll wrappers and filling.

4. Deep-fry the spring rolls in 3 to 4 batches, cooking them until they are golden brown and crispy (about 3 minutes). Remove with a slotted spoon, and drain on paper towels.

Easy Chinese

Xǐshǒujiān zài nǎr?
洗手间 在哪儿?
Where is the restroom?

Jiézhàng.
结账。
The bill, please.

责任编辑：彭　博
英文编辑：郭　辉　张　乐
封面设计：战文婷
印刷监制：佟汉冬

图书在版编目（CIP）数据

我爱中国菜：英文 / 吉暐编著.—北京：华语教学出版社，2009
ISBN 978-7-80200-644-7

Ⅰ. 我… Ⅱ. 吉… Ⅲ. 菜谱－中国－英文 Ⅳ. TS972.182

中国版本图书馆CIP数据核字（2009）第159824号

我爱中国菜

吉暐　编著
*

©华语教学出版社有限责任公司
华语教学出版社有限责任公司出版
（中国北京百万庄大街24号 邮政编码100037）
电话：(86)10-68320585　68997826
传真：(86)10-68997826　68326333
网址：www.sinolingua.com.cn
电子信箱：hyjx@sinolingua.com.cn
新浪微博地址：http://weibo.com/sinolinguavip
大厂回族自治县德诚印务有限公司印刷
2009年（大32开）第1版
2014年第4次印刷
（英文）
ISBN 978-7-80200-644-7
定价：48.00元